Countdown to Christmas

Written by Susie Starr

Design and Layout by Sara Marie Qualls

Copyright © 2013 by Susie Starr

COUNTDOWN TO CHRISTMAS

by Susie Starr

Printed in the United States of America

ISBN 9781628397154

All rights reserved solely by the author. The author guarantees all contents are original and do not infringe upon the legal rights of any other person or work. No part of this book may be reproduced in any form without the permission of the author. The views expressed in this book are not necessarily those of the publisher.

Unless otherwise indicated, Bible quotations are taken from the New International Version (NIV). Copyright © 1973, 1978, 1984, 2011 by Biblica, Inc.™ . Used by permission. All rights reserved.

www.xulonpress.com

DEDICATION

This book is dedicated with love to my grandchildren.

Scott, for whom the book was written, Kyle, Gary,
Noelle, Madison, Jack, Caleb, Gwyne and Hannah.

You have filled my life with joy.
I pray that your sense of family will always be strong
and that as you grow you will cherish our family ties.
My heart's desire is that you will love and serve
The Lord with all your heart, soul, mind and strength.

And one day, should The Lord tarry, you will
Countdown to Christmas with your
own children and tell them about your Grammy
and the story we shared.

Acknowledgements

I want to thank my husband, Kim Starr, for his love, support and insistence that this book be published. You truly are the wind beneath my wings! Thank you for your constant and steady love. You are simply the best! You have spoiled me, the girls, and our grandchildren with your lavish patience and generous love.

To my precious daughters, Kimberly and Heather, I say thank you for the joy you have given me as I have watched you grow into the women that you are today. Without struggle there is no growth. The butterfly must struggle to break free from the cocoon. It is the struggle that gives it the strength to fly. I have treasured watching you grow and I love watching you fly!

And to my parents, Jack and Lavonne Coleburn, who have changed their address from earth to Heaven, there are no words to express my gratitude for my godly heritage. I am very grateful for their influence in my life. I would love for Jesus to tell them that this book is finally published. I know they would be proud!

To Rebekah and Sara, my deepest gratitude for your encouragement and help with pulling this all together!
Thank God for "Divine appointments!"

The acknowledgement of the countless people who have influenced my life and supported me on my journey could fill not a page, but volumes. So I give thanks to The Lord who placed each precious friend, helper, and encourager in my life.
To God be the glory for the things He has done!

ORNAMENTS

Day 1...The Angel Gabriel
Day 2...Mary
Day 3...Joseph
Day 4...The Donkey
Day 5...Bethlehem
Day 6...The Inn/No Room
Day 7...The Stable
Day 8...Baby Jesus
Day 9...The Manger
Day 10...The Shepherds
Day 11...The Lamb
Day 12...The Angel
Day 13...The Multitude of Angels
Day 14...The Star
Day 15...The Crown
Day 16...The Wise Men
Day 17...The World
Day 18...The Christmas Tree
Day 19...Santa
Day 20...A Church
Day 21...Cookies
Day 22...The Wreath
Day 23...The Carolers
Day 24...Cookies for Santa
Day 25...Happy Birthday Jesus

Introduction

   As a young wife and mother, I was determined to make the most of the time that I had with my children creating memories and weaving a sense of family and tradition into the fabric of their lives. I read books, went to seminars and took classes. You name it, I did it! Whenever I would introduce something new, my kids would roll their eyes, shake their heads, laugh and say, "Mom's been to another seminar!" That's okay, it worked! A sense of security and belonging filled our home. Traditions create stability and a sense of well being in a child's heart. When our first grandchild, Scott, was born, a new sense of excitement grew in my heart as I realized that I would have the opportunity to establish new traditions that we would share together.

We had the wonderful privilege of having Scott live next door to us, so I was able to be very involved in his early years. He was two years old, we were getting ready for the Christmas season. His eyes were all aglow with the wonder of it all! Then it hit me! I had to seize the moment and teach this little guy what Christmas was all about. As the ideas flooded my heart, I asked my husband, Kim, to go out into the garage and build me a tree. I gave him the design I had in my head, and off he went! A few hours later he returned with just what I wanted! Now for the next step in my plan, to teach Scott about Christmas. I sat down and wrote a little book. Each day beginning on December 1st we would read the page for the day and hang an ornament on the tree that Papa had made. I quickly gathered and made ornaments that would correspond to the daily theme. On December 1st my little guy and I sat by our tree and began to countdown the days until Christmas. We would tell and retell the story each day as we added ornaments to the tree. Scott quickly learned about the angel, Mary, Joseph, the shepherds, wisemen and most of all about baby Jesus. He would recite to me the story everyday as we added the next ornament I can't tell you how much joy flooded my heart each day as he told me the story! When Christmas finally arrived my two year old grandson could recite the Christmas story just as I had written it in our little book.

Introduction

That year we began a family tradition that has become a central part of our Christmas. It has been shared with nine precious grandchildren over the course of eighteen years. We don't all live next door to each other any more, but every Christmas we still share the tradition. My daughters set up their own trees, made by Papa, haul out the ornaments that have been passed down and gathered and each day we countdown to Christmas! My prayer is that you will enjoy making this a part of your family's Christmas traditions for many generations to come.
Merry Christmas!

Susie Starr

December 1st

The angel Gabriel came to a young woman named Mary. He had good news for her, but she was afraid. The angel said, "Fear not…"

The Angel Gabriel

Have you ever been afraid?
God promises to be with us always. Fear Not!

December 2nd

The good news that Gabriel brought to Mary was that she was going to have a baby. Her baby would be God's son. He would save the world from their sins. What exciting news!

Mary

Ask your Mom or Dad to tell you about the day that they found out you were "on the way". That was exciting news!

December 3rd

The angel Gabriel was busy! He went to Joseph, the man that Mary was engaged to marry. He told Joseph not to be afraid to marry Mary. Her baby would be God's son.

God chose Joseph to be his son's earthly father. Joseph was a good man. He was a carpenter. What is your dad's job?

December 4th

It was almost time for Mary's baby to be born. Mary and Joseph had to travel to Bethlehem, Joseph's hometown. It was a long trip. Mary rode on a donkey.

The Donkey

Have you ever been on a long trip? Talk about your memories. Thank God for his protection as you travel.

December 5th

Bethlehem was Joseph's hometown. Because the governor wanted to count all the people from Bethlehem, Mary and Joseph had to go there.

Do you know the name of the city you live in?
Today would be a good day to work on learning your address.

December 6th

Because so many people had to travel to Bethlehem to be counted, the city was very crowded. Mary and Joseph could not find a place to stay.

The Inn/No Room

Thank God for your nice home. Pray for others who are homeless and hungry. How could you help them?

December 7th

Because there was no room for them in the Inn, Mary and Joseph stayed in a stable with the animals.

The Stable

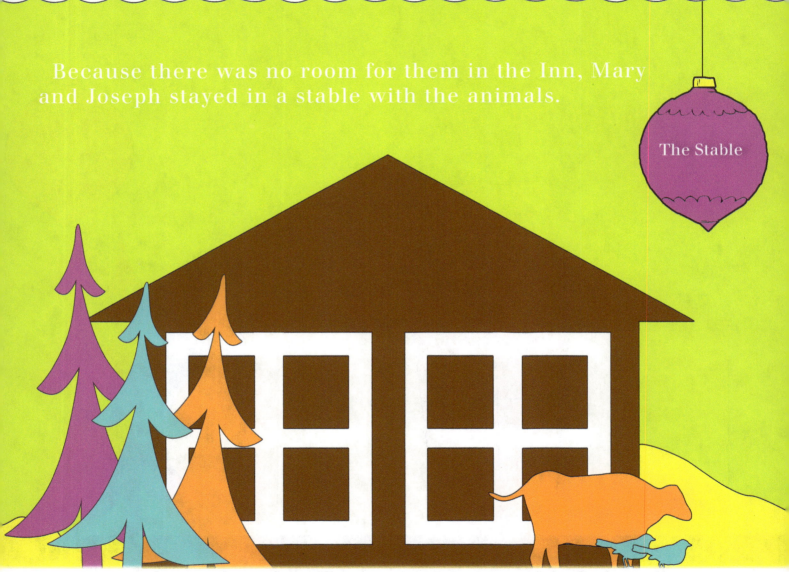

Name some animals that might have been in the stable.
What is your favorite animal? Thank God for all His creatures.

December 8th

While Mary and Joseph were in the stable in Bethlehem, Mary's baby was born. She named him Jesus. His name means, "God with us". God sent Jesus to show us what He is like.

Baby Jesus

What does your name mean?
Ask your parents how they chose your name.

December 9th

Mary wrapped Jesus up in a soft piece of cloth. Because she had no cradle for him in the stable, Mary laid Jesus in the manger.

The Manger

Can you sing the song *Away In A Manger*?

December 10th

On the night that Jesus was born, there were shepherds on the hills near Bethlehem watching their sheep. Jesus is sometimes called "The Good Shepherd" because He takes such good care of us.

The Shepherds

Jesus is the good shepherd and you are his little lamb.
Thank him for taking such good care of you.

December 11th

Even though Jesus is "The Good Shepherd" he is sometimes called "The Lamb of God". When he grew up his cousin, John the Baptist, called him "The Lamb of God who takes away the sin of the world."

The Lamb

Jesus came to this world to forgive us of our sins.
Do you know what sin is? The Bible says we have all sinned.

December 12th

Suddenly an angel of the Lord appeared to the shepherds and said, "Look! I'm bringing you news of great joy! A savior has been born in Bethlehem. You will find him lying in a manger."

The Angel

What do you think the shepherds did when the angel said this?
Draw a picture of the angel and the shepherds.

December 13th

All at once the sky grew bright with a multitude of angels. They were all praising God and singing, "Glory to God in the highest, and on earth peace, goodwill to all men."

The Multitude of Angels

Jesus came to bring peace to the world. Pray for our world.
Thank God for the peaceful life you have.

December 14th

The night that Jesus was born, a new star appeared in the sky. The Bible tells us that the star stood over the place where Jesus was born.

The Star

Every star in the sky was put there by God.
Go outside tonight and do a little star gazing.

December 15th

Three wise men saw the new star and knew that it meant a new King had been born. Jesus is sometimes called "The King of Kings and the Lord of Lords."

The Crown

Get out the art supplies and make a crown.
One day all who love Jesus will wear a crown in Heaven.

December 16th

The three wise men followed the star to where Jesus was. They brought him gifts of gold, frankincense, and myrrh. This is why we give gifts at Christmas.

The Wise Men

What gift could you give Jesus today?
The best gift to give him is your heart.

December 17th

"For God so loved the world he gave his one and only son, that whoever believes in him shall not perish but have eternal life." - John 3:16

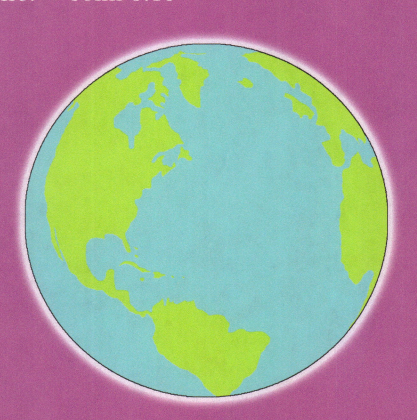

The World

Do you believe in Jesus? He loves you so much that He gave his life for you. Memorize John 3:16.

December 18th

At Christmas we put up a Christmas tree. It reminds us of God's love because it is evergreen. We remember that Jesus died on a cross made of wood...a tree.

The Christmas Tree

Thank Jesus for giving His life for you.
Have you decorated your Christmas tree yet?

December 19th

A long time ago there was a man named Saint Nicholas. He loved Jesus and showed God's love by giving gifts to the poor. God gave us His greatest gift when He sent Jesus.

Santa

Do you know someone you could show God's love to today? What could you do to show them God's love?

December 20th

Christmas is a very special time to worship the Lord. The Bible tells us to get together with others who believe in Jesus and worship Him. This is why we go to church.

A Church

Make sure to go to church this Christmas and thank God for sending Jesus. Invite a friend to come along.

DECEMBER 21ST

At Christmas we enjoy sharing good food with our family and friends. Special treats like cookies and hot chocolate are so much fun to enjoy.

Cookies

What is your favorite Christmas food?
Make a batch of Christmas cookies and share them with a friend.

December 22nd

At Christmas time we decorate our houses and put a wreath on the door to say "Welcome!" to every one who comes by. Christmas is a special time to be with family and friends.

The Wreath

Is there a wreath on your door? Invite a friend to come over and make them feel welcome! Jesus welcomes all of us.

December 23rd

Joy to the world, the Lord has come! Let Earth receive her king. Let every heart prepare Him room. And heaven and nature sing!

The Carolers

Listen to your favorite Christmas music today. Don't forget to hum along! Maybe you could go caroling.

December 24th

There is only one more day until Christmas! Make sure your stocking is hung, put out some milk and cookies for Santa, and don't forget to say your prayers! Remember that with all the fun, Christmas is about Jesus. He is the reason for the season.

Cookies for Santa

Read a favorite Christmas story before going to bed tonight. Go to sleep quickly! Tomorrow is Christmas Day!

DECEMBER 25TH

Happy Birthday Jesus! And Merry Christmas to you my little friend. Have the best Christmas ever! You have counted down all the days and you know the story of why we celebrate very well. Enjoy the celebration!

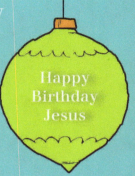

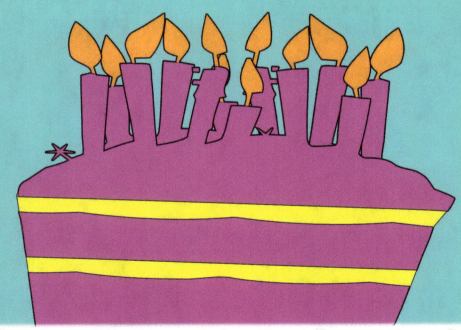

Tell the Christmas story one more time. Pray now and thank God for all of his blessings...especially for sending Jesus.

Tree Diagram

Supplies:
1 - 2x2x4' Douglas Fir
2 - 2x2x18" Douglas Fir
4 - 1x4-45 degree braces or metal angle brackets
1 - 1x4x31½" pine (ends cut at 65 + or - degrees)
1 - 1x4x22" pine (ends cut to above angle)
1 - 1x4x12x¾" pine (ends cut to above angle)
1 - 1x4x at 3¼"
15 - #6 x 1⅜" drywall screws (or similar screws)
2 - #6 2¼ or 2½ drywall screw to attach base to upright
25 - small cup hooks
Numbers - 1 through 25
Paint

Cut all the pieces to length. Rabbit the 2x2x4' and 2x2x18" pieces to dimensions given. Cut angles on cross pieces. Cup hooks should be placed ½" up, spaced at 2¼' apart, beginning in the center of the board (top- 2 cup hooks, next- 5 hooks, next- 7 hooks, next- 11 hooks). Use a nail to make pilot holes for hooks. Assemble all pieces with screws. Paint the tree. Place hooks in piloted holes. Place numbers above appropriate hooks.

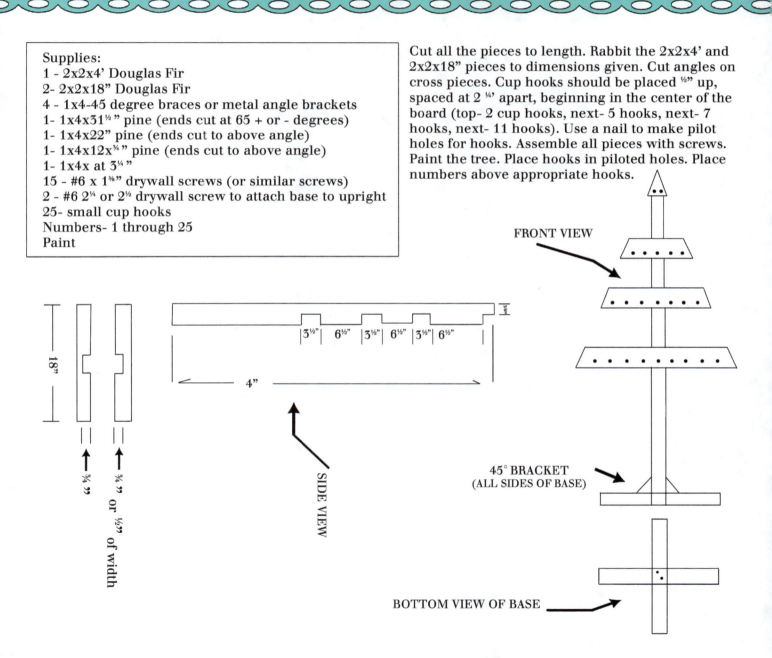

About the Author

Susie Starr is a preacher's daughter who grew up to be a preacher's wife. Living her entire life surrounded by ministry Susie heard God's call on her heart at a very early age. A gifted ventriloquist, Susie began public speaking at the age of 16. She has been a featured camp and retreat speaker for over 42 years. Using her gifts of humor and music, Susie has ministered to audiences of all ages with a message of contagious faith. Her greatest love in life is her family. Serving The Lord along side of her husband Kim in pastoral ministry for 40 years and raising their two daughters has been her greatest journey. The proud "Grammy" of nine, Susie continues to enthusiastically share the love of The Lord and sense of family with, as she calls them, The Big Ones, The Middle Ones and the Little Ones. Firmly believing that there is no greater joy in life than to teach a child to love The Lord with all their heart, soul, mind and strength.

Printed in the USA
CPSIA information can be obtained
at www.ICGtesting.com
LVHW081010191123
764237LV00075B/1336